SCROLL S...

MILITARY DESIGNS

Patterns For All Branches of the U.S. Military

by Mike and Vicky Lewis

Fox Chapel Publishing Co. Inc.

1970 Broad Street • East Petersburg, PA 17520 • www.carvingworld.com

Publisher:	Alan Giagnocavo
Project Editor:	Ayleen Stellhorn
Desktop Specialist:	Linda L. Eberly, Eberly Designs Inc.

ISBN # 1-56523-146-5

To order your copy of this book,
please send check or money order
for $9.95 plus $3.00 shipping to:
Fox Books
1970 Broad Street
East Petersburg, PA 17520

Or visit us on the web at
www.carvingworld.com

Manufactured in the USA

This book is dedicated . . .

. . . to all the men and women who have served our country, to the families of those who have served, and to all the servicemen and women currently enlisted, so that all people can enjoy the freedom they so joyfully have each day.

. . . in loving memory of Mike's Uncle James Phillips, an Army Infantry Veteran and Silver Star recipient from the Vietnam War.

. . . to Mike's stepfather, Howard "Doc" Kash, a Navy Veteran from the Korean Conflict and World War II.

TABLE OF CONTENTS

ABOUT THE AUTHORS

Mike and Vicky Lewis

Mike Lewis, an Army Veteran, has been perfecting his scroll saw techniques since 1987. What started as a hobby for Mike has now become a very rewarding career, progressing from basic scroll work projects to recreating his own designs and teaching.

Vicky began scrolling in 1998 to help Mike. This quickly became a passion for her. Cutting almost daily, she quickly realized their scroll saw could be used not only to cut elegant Victorian scroll work, but also to cut the many wood items and personal designs that are displayed in their shop.

Currently, both Mike and Vicky are demonstrating craftsmen and teachers at Dollywood Theme Park in Pigeon Forge, Tennessee. Their shop, Sawdust and Shavings, is located in the Mountain Crafts Marketplace in Craftsman's Valley inside the park. For more information about classes and scroll work, contact Mike and Vicky directly at (865) 428-9401 ext. 2259 or e-mail them at *mlewis58@bellsouth.net*.

HELPFUL HINTS

Listed below are suggested and helpful hints that can be used when cutting the designs in this book. Use whatever materials, sizes and techniques best suit your needs.

Materials

We suggest 1/8 in. to 1/4 in. birch plywood or Baltic birch plywood, along with any hardwood. Select your wood with care. Wood should be "clean" on both sides. We do not suggest using pine to cut any of the designs shown in this book.

Design Layout

There are several methods that can be used to lay out the designs in this book. You can use the method suggested here or one that you find has worked well for you in the past.

First, always make a photocopy of the original design you are going to cut. This saves your master copy for future use. You can reduce or enlarge the designs as necessary on a photocopier or by scanning the pattern into a computer program that will allow you to scale the design.

Then, use a repositioning spray glue on the back side of the pattern to adhere the design to the face of the wood. We recommend Super 77™ spray glue, a 3M product. You can determine the "face" of the wood by looking for the best grain lines and no flaws. Caution: Lightly spray the paper only.

Blades

We use #5, #2 and #2/0 reverse teeth blades. The reverse teeth blades help keep the wood from fraying on the back side and clean up any inside cut areas. The #2/0R saw blades are used to cut all accent and detail lines in all of the designs, ie: wings and other areas indicated by solid black lines.

Cutting Tips

Depending on the material thickness, stack two to four pieces of wood at a time. Secure the pieces with nail brads placed in each of the four corners of the wood and in scrap areas to be cut out. Secure one corner with three brads to form a triangle in that corner.

As a general rule, cut the most delicate areas first. This includes all the accent and detail lines in each design. Solid lines outside the cut areas indicating

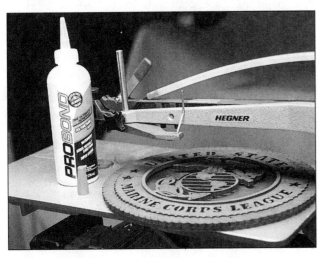

A good wood glue, such as Pro Bond, and a rich stain are two of the materials needed to complete the designs in this book. You'll also need spray glue to hold the pattern down. The authors recommend using #5, #2 and #2/0 reverse teeth blades to cut the patterns.

Small wood spacers are inserted between the layers of the design to give the final piece added dimension.

accent or detail lines should be cut also.

Cut out all areas marked with an "x." Leave cuts marked with an arrow until last, cutting away the center circle first and then the inside rope area.

Cutting in a counter-clockwise motion and starting at the triangle corner, begin cutting the outside rope area around to the halfway point. Cut the scrap away and add in the detail line that defines the rope.

Begin cutting the second half of the outside rope, also in a counter-clockwise motion, up to the corner with the three nails. You should have approximately three to seven cuts left after the accent lines have been cut.

Begin cutting the remaining section in a clockwise motion, making sure to cut the accent lines at the same time that you are making the scalloped cut. Continue cutting until the rope has been completely cut away from the corner.

Finishing Tips

Remove the pattern carefully from the wood. Use a pocket knife to gently lift a pattern that is difficult to remove.

Sand and stain the finished piece to suit. We use MinWax™ products.

After the piece has dried, reassemble the three rings by turning the pieces face down. The second ring is elevated by small $1/8$ in. pieces of wood called spacers. Use at least four spacers to elevate this ring. The outside rope is elevated by $1/4$ in. spacers. Use at least four spacers to elevate this ring also. The center ring lies flat on the work surface.

Glue along each ring edge. Let the glue dry completely before lifting the piece. We use ProBond™ wood glue, an Elmer's Glue product, to glue wood surfaces.

A wood back can be added to the back of any design to add color and dimension to your cut piece. Be sure the diameter of this back is cut small enough to fit inside the scallops of the rope-cut edge.

Pieces can also be placed in shadow boxes.

Personalization

Each design can be personalized using the alphabet circle and the number circle located in the back of this book. Try adding a service member's name and rank. You can also add dates of service and other personal information. There are many more designations that can be spelled out as well.

When you personalize a design, make sure the names and ranks, along with dates and other personal information, are centered to guarantee total balance in the design.

United States Air Force

© Mike and Vicky Lewis

© Mike and Vicky Lewis

AIR FORCE

United States Air Force Retired

© Mike and Vicky Lewis

United States Air Force Reserve

© Mike and Vicky Lewis

© Mike and Vicky Lewis

© Mike and Vicky Lewis

United States Air Force blank design

United States Army

© Mike and Vicky Lewis

United States Army Veteran

© Mike and Vicky Lewis

United States Army Retired

© Mike and Vicky Lewis

© Mike and Vicky Lewis

United States Army Reserve

© Mike and Vicky Lewis

© Mike and Vicky Lewis

United States Army Recruiter

© Mike and Vicky Lewis

United States Army Aviation

© Mike and Vicky Lewis

United States Army Air Corps

© Mike and Vicky Lewis

United States Army Rangers

© Mike and Vicky Lewis

U.S. Army Special Forces

© Mike and Vicky Lewis

U.S. Special Forces Green Beret

© Mike and Vicky Lewis

ARMY

United States Army blank design

© Mike and Vicky Lewis

© Mike and Vicky Lewis

COAST GUARD

United States Coast Guard Veteran

© Mike and Vicky Lewis

United States Coast Guard Retired

© Mike and Vicky Lewis

COAST GUARD

United States Coast Guard blank design

© Mike and Vicky Lewis

SEMPER FIDELIS

UNITED STATES

MARINE CORPS

© Mike and Vicky Lewis

United States Marine Corps Veteran

© Mike and Vicky Lewis

United States Marine Corps Retired

SEMPER FIDELIS

UNITED STATES

MARINE CORPS RETIRED

© Mike and Vicky Lewis

United States Marine Corps Reserve

SEMPER FIDELIS

© Mike and Vicky Lewis

SEMPER FIDELIS

© Mike and Vicky Lewis

United States Marine Corps Aviation

© Mike and Vicky Lewis

United States Marine Corps Recon

SEMPER FIDELIS

UNITED STATES

MARINE CORPS RECON

© Mike and Vicky Lewis

UNITED STATES

MARINE CORPS RECON

United States Marine Corps blank design

SEMPER FIDELIS

United States Navy

© Mike and Vicky Lewis

NAVY

United States Navy Veteran

© Mike and Vicky Lewis

United States Navy Retired

© Mike and Vicky Lewis

United States Navy Reserve

United States Navy Submarine Service

© Mike and Vicky Lewis

Scroll Saw Military Designs

United States Navy Recruiting Command

© Mike and Vicky Lewis

NAVY

United States Navy Seal Team

© Mike and Vicky Lewis

United States Naval Aviation

© Mike and Vicky Lewis

United States Navy blank design

U.S. Navy Seabee

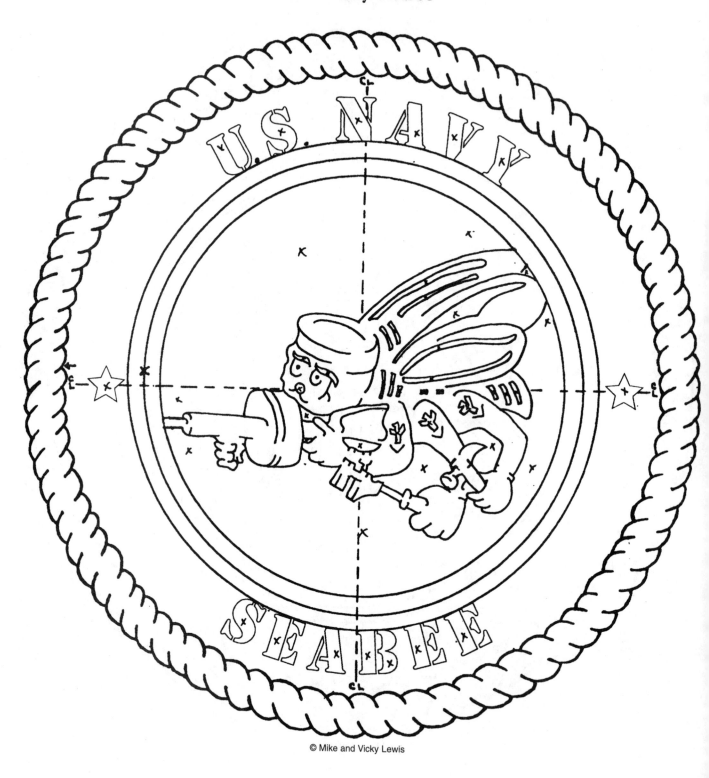

© Mike and Vicky Lewis

NAVY SEABEE

U.S. Navy Seabee Veteran

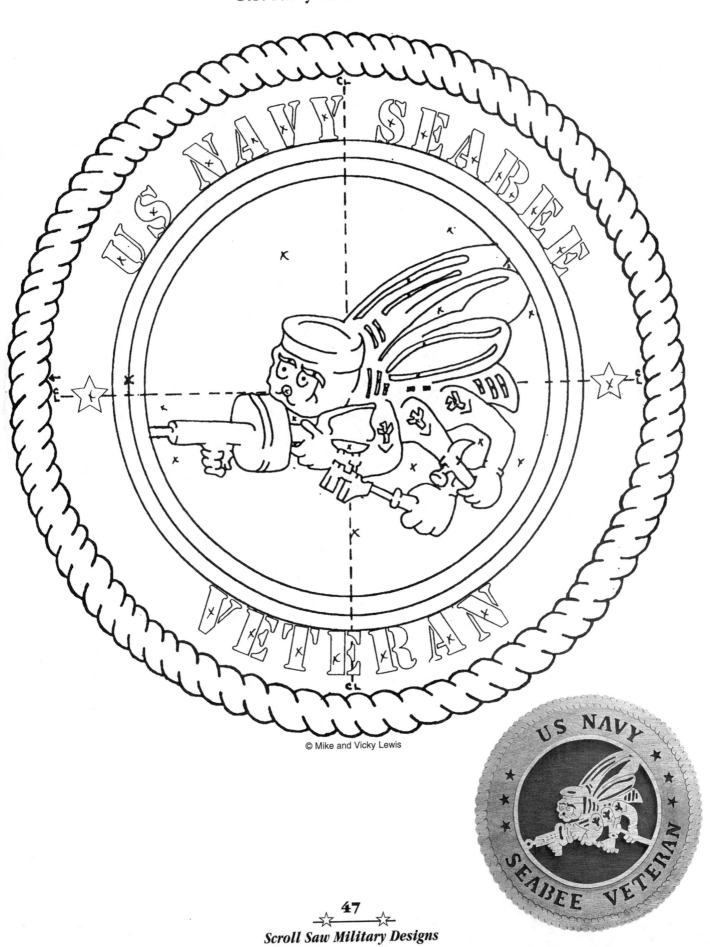

© Mike and Vicky Lewis

U.S. Navy Seabee Retired

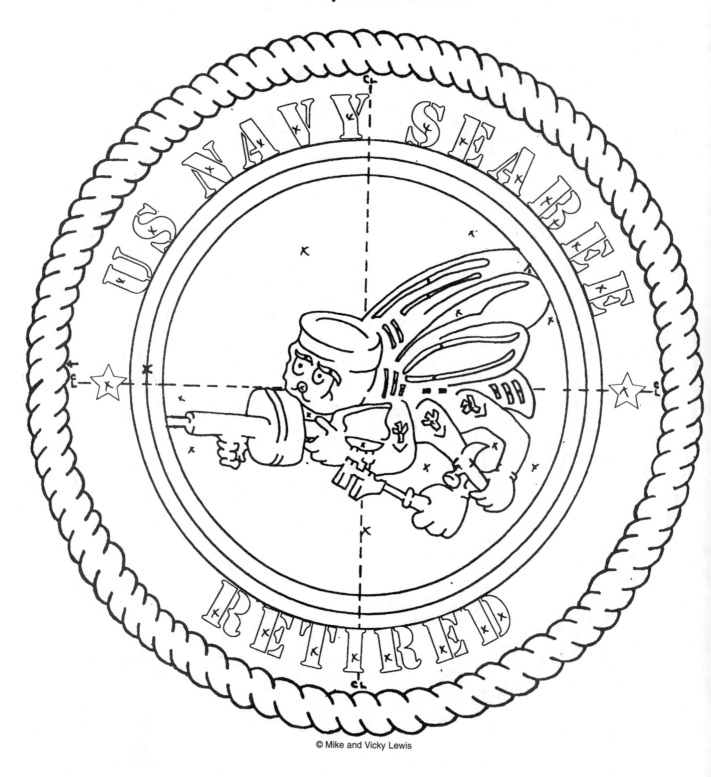

© Mike and Vicky Lewis

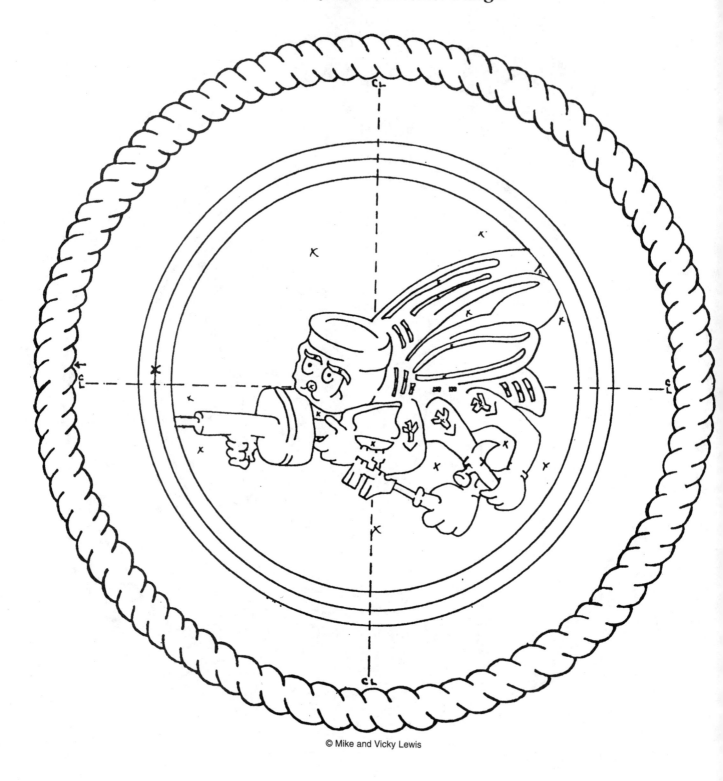

© Mike and Vicky Lewis

POW-MIA

POW-MIA Not Forgotten plaque

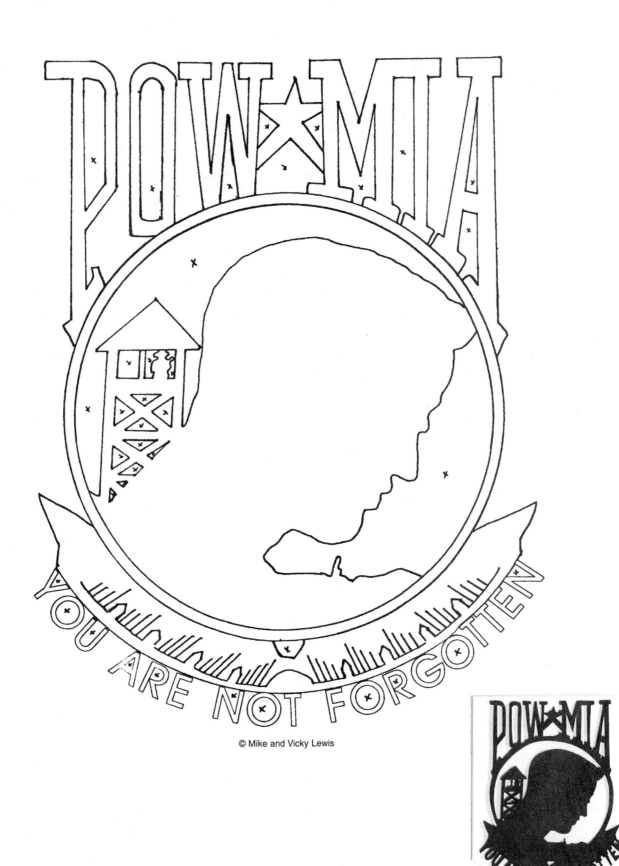

© Mike and Vicky Lewis

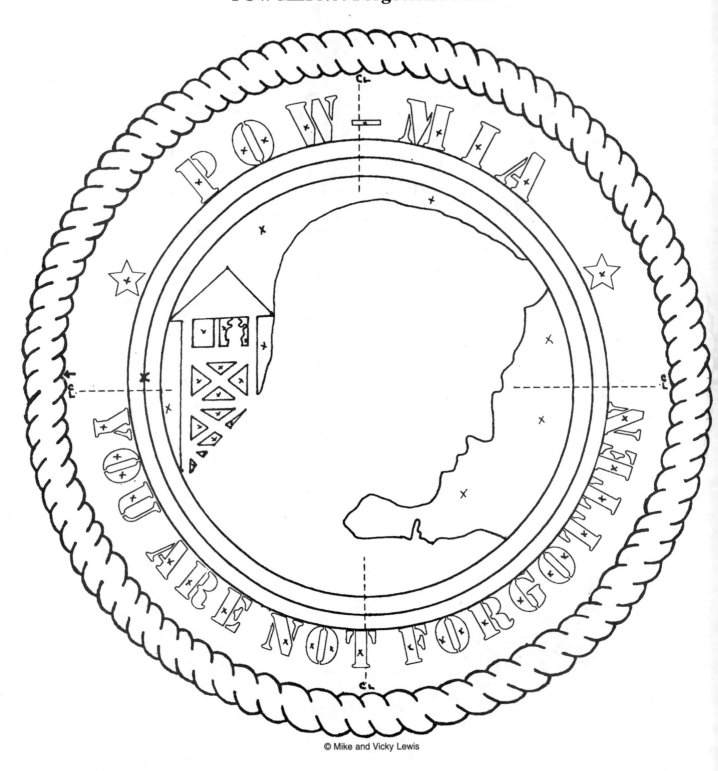

© Mike and Vicky Lewis

MILITARY POLICE

United States Military Police

© Mike and Vicky Lewis

Use the words and seals in this section to create designs for veterans of foreign wars. For example, "Desert Storm Veteran" can be placed around any of the six seals on pages 56, 57 and 58. With this method, you can easily create veteran plaques for Army, Air Force, Coast Guard, Marines, Navy and Navy Seabee for each of the five conflicts listed in this section. You can also personalize these designs by using the alphabet and number circles on pages 59 and 60.

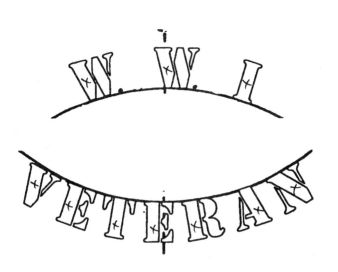

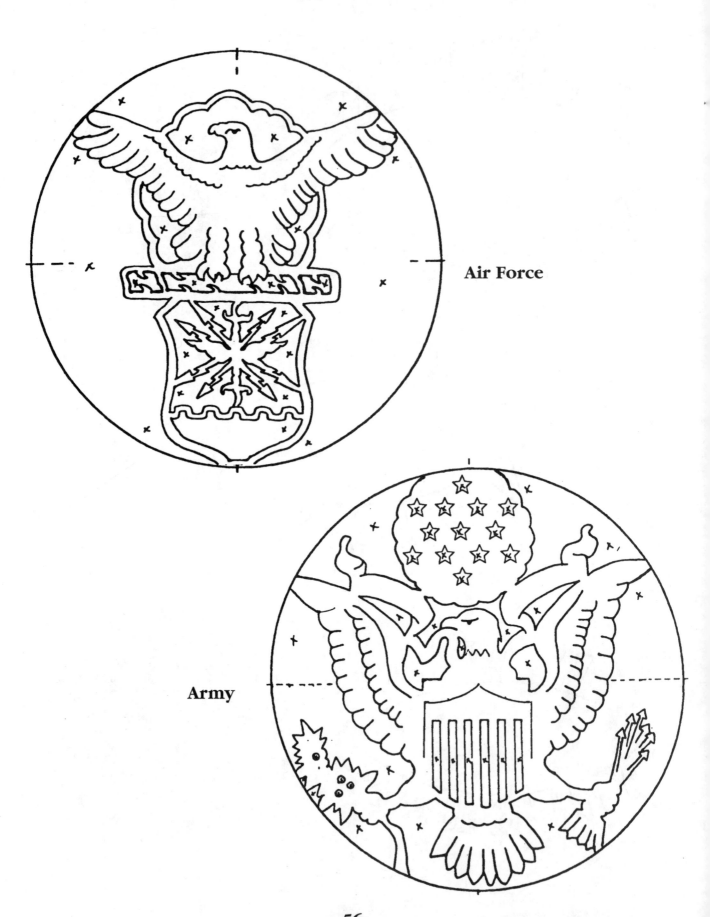

Air Force

Army

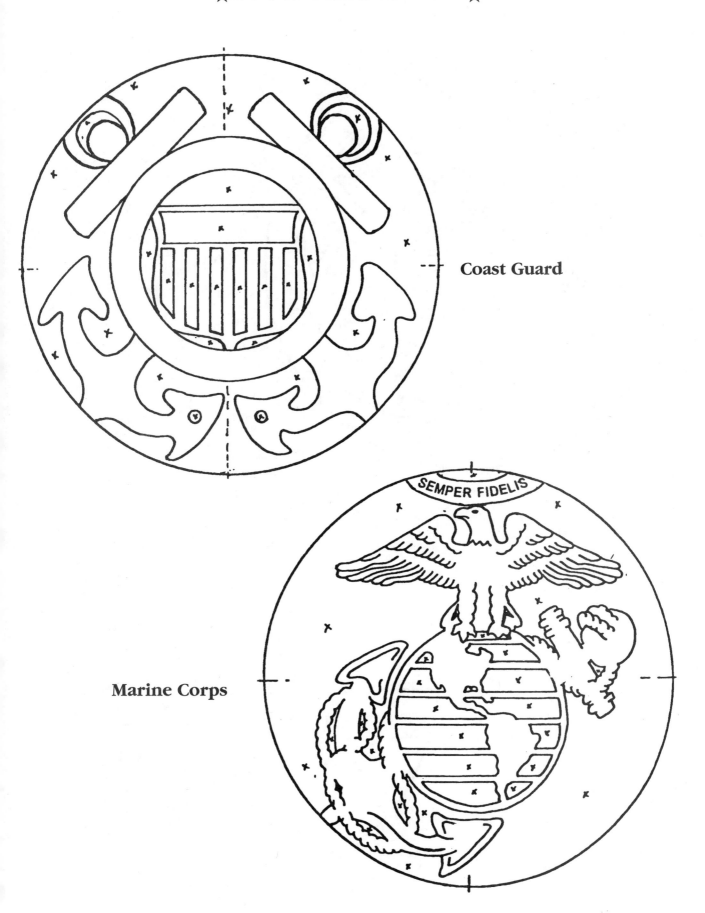

Coast Guard

Marine Corps

SEMPER FIDELIS

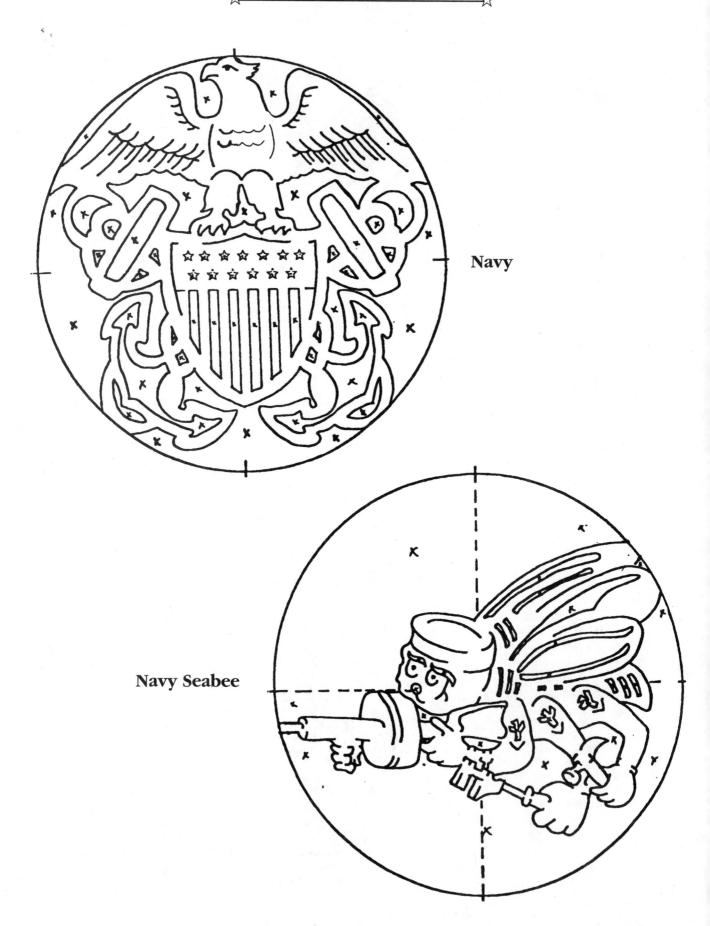

Navy

Navy Seabee

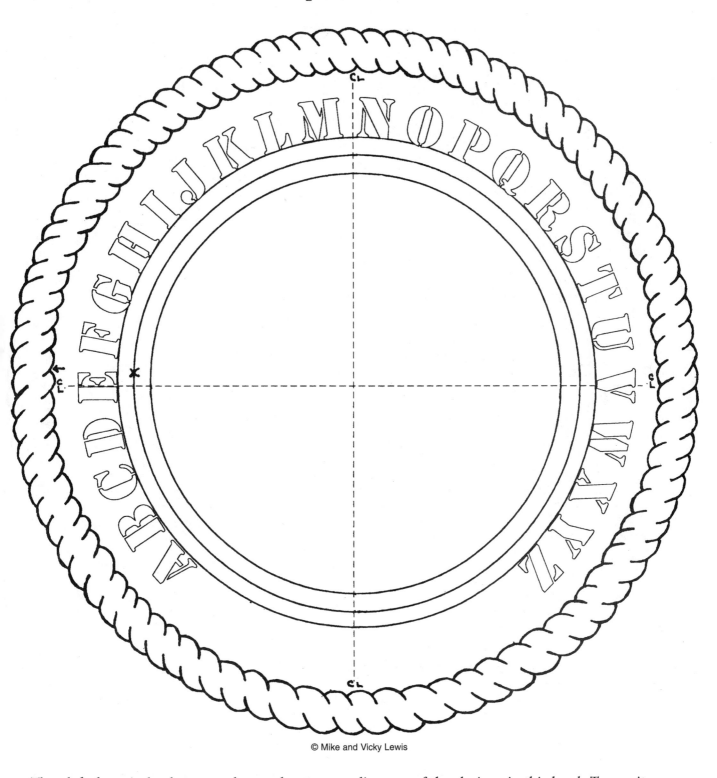

The alphabet circle above can be used to personalize any of the designs in this book. To use it, copy this page as many times as needed, taking into account any duplicate letters in your new design. Cut and paste the letters on the blank design circles (Air Force, page 10; Army, page 23; Coast Guard, page 27; Marine Corps, page 36; Navy, page 45). Add numbers from the number and star circle on page 60. Copy your completed design, and you are ready to begin cutting on the saw.

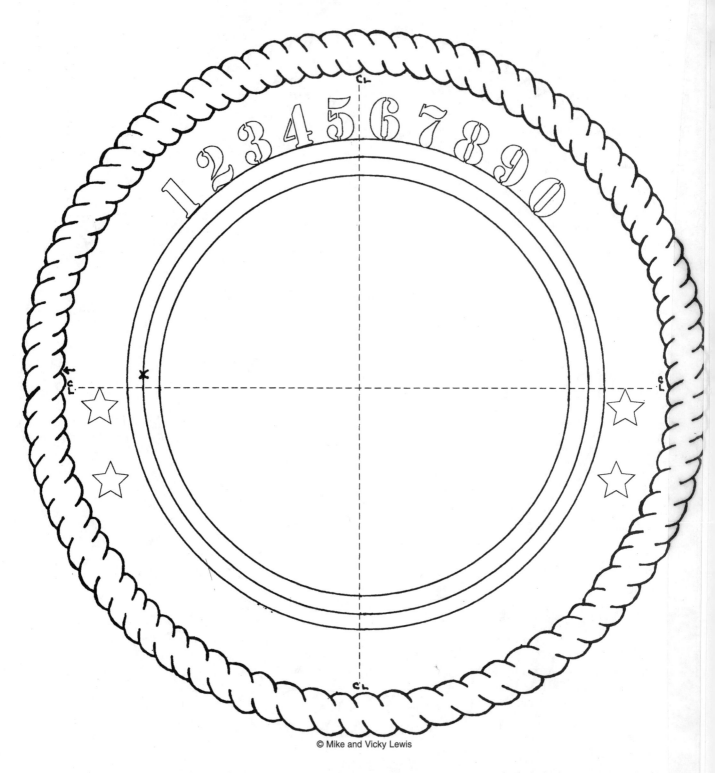

© Mike and Vicky Lewis

The number and star circle above can be used in the same manner as the alphabet circle on the previous page to personalize any of the designs in this book. To use it, copy this page as many times as needed, taking into account any duplicate numbers in your new design. Cut and paste the numbers on the blank design circles (Air Force, page 10; Army, page 23; Coast Guard, page 27; Marine Corps, page 36; Navy, page 45). Add letters from the alphabet circle on page 59. Copy your completed design, and you are ready to begin cutting on the saw.